Sensual
MASSAGE

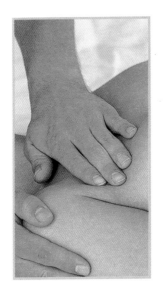

Sensual
MASSAGE

Susan Mumford

hamlyn

An Hachette Livre UK Company
This edition first published in Great Britain in 2002 by Hamlyn,
a division of Octopus Publishing Group Ltd
2–4 Heron Quays, London E14 4JP

Distributed in the United States and Canada by
Sterling Publishing Co., Inc.
387 Park Avenue South, New York, NY 10016–8810

ISBN-13: 978 0 600 60619 2
ISBN-10: 0 600 60619 8

A CIP catalogue record for this book is available at the
British Library

Printed and bound in Hong Kong

10 9 8 7 6 5 4

The material in this book has been adapted
from the following title previously published by Hamlyn:
Sensual Massage: A Lover's Guide 2001

CONTENTS

INTRODUCTION

We love to touch. We are tactile, sensual beings. We perceive the world through our senses – sight, sound, taste, touch, smell – and out of all of them, touching perhaps affects us the most deeply.

Touch communicates, brings closeness, restores and arouses. From infancy, we use touch to find out about the world, to explore, reach out and confirm. Through touch we are able to affirm or transform our relationships. Touch tells us who we are, it gives us a sense of ourselves, allows us to make contact and feel we are not alone. We use touch for pleasure, to bring relationships closer, to comfort and accept.

Our senses and feelings can give us balance and satisfaction. They are an antidote to a thinking, technical world. In order to find such a balance, we need to focus our senses and examine our surroundings. We need an environment where we can feel, let go, open up emotionally, receive pleasure and relax, taking care to have around us objects that we like, inspiring shapes, softness and curves.

In exploring the sensual world we naturally increase our use of touch. Touching our surroundings, the people we encounter, those we are close to, and those we love.

The way that we, as lovers, touch defines the bond between us. Through sensuality we explore each other, heightening both arousal and awareness. Pleasing each other, we increase our sense of loving and being loved.

THE BEAUTY OF MASSAGE

Massage celebrates sensuality. It is an experience of giving and receiving, of exploring and opening to each other. It is a way of pleasing and relaxing, releasing stress and tension, and creates a profound feeling of wellbeing. In getting to know each other better, we increase the trust and sharing vital for a loving relationship to thrive. The wonderful thing about massage is that it feels as good to give as receive.

Massage can be used for simple relaxation – as a way of easing tired muscles, calming the mind, uplifting the spirit and restoring our natural energy. Doing this for our partner gives a special satisfaction. For our partner, allowing a caring touch to discover and ease away tensions is a statement of openness and their trust in us.

A FEELING OF INTIMACY

Intimate massage combines basic massage techniques, designed to relax and keep muscles healthy, with added sensual arousal and the spontaneity of loving touch. With sensual massage, each one pleasures and satisfies the other, creating an intimate, loving, two-way flow. There is no right way to do it, it depends on a shared experience. If our attention is on our partner, we will be concerned only with their happiness, and a tender sensitivity will develop. The beauty of a sensual massage is that it enhances our relationship, by increasing knowledge, vitality and joy.

The sensual massage in this book will take you about an hour to give. If you don't have a full hour, concentrate on one particular area, giving it your full loving attention.

PREPARING FOR MASSAGE

Preparing for sensual massage can be a sensual experience in itself. It sets the mood, and the care and thought put into it will increase your enjoyment of the massage. Take time with your partner to gently relax your body. Allow your mind to clear, let go of any preoccupations, focusing your thoughts on your partner and yourself. Gentle breathing and body sensing, followed by muscle relaxation, will help increase your inner balance.

First, prepare the oil that you will use for the massage. You need a 'carrier' or 'base' oil, the basic oil used to allow the hands to glide freely over the skin. Grapeseed, a light vegetable oil without a heavy smell, is an excellent carrier oil. Almond oil, a slightly sweeter, thicker oil, feels more luxurious on the skin. Oils of avocado and apricot are rich, nourishing oils, while oil of jojoba is a beautiful, more expensive oil, which is particularly good for massaging the face. You can mix two carrier oils to make your basic oil, for example use grapeseed oil with 10 per cent almond oil added.

ESSENTIAL OILS

Another group of oils, essential oils, are added to the carrier oil to enhance the effect of massage. Containing the essential nature of a plant, they are extremely potent, and you need only use a few drops. Traditionally essential oils are used for the treatment of various conditions and they should not be used undiluted on the skin. For example, for relaxation use lavender, a particularly useful fresh, healing oil, or camomile, which has a calming, sedative effect. In order to get to know the oils, try them separately, mixing a couple of drops into some base oil.

THE RIGHT OIL FOR YOU

For heightening sensual arousal, try oils known as aphrodisiacs – sandalwood, a woody, sedating, eastern scent; patchouli, a more stimulating, sweet, dark odour; or ylang ylang, which has a euphoric, sweet, floral smell. Experiment with these different oils and see which ones attract you.

Perhaps the most beautiful of oils, and also the most expensive, are delicate neroli (orange blossom), which sedates; exotic jasmine, which uplifts; and luxurious, soothing oil of rose. Also reputed to have aphrodisiac properties, these are evocative, irresistibly heady scents. On pages 124–5 you will find a list of oils and their properties and some recipes for you to try out. Although mixing can be extremely satisfying, you can if you prefer buy ready mixed oils.

There are various oils that you can use, and finding a combination that suits you is often just a matter of experimentation. You can make up as much as you like. If you start with 28ml (1fl oz) of base oil you will make enough oil for about four massages. The ratio you should remember is use up to, but not more than, 12 drops of essential oil per 28ml (1fl oz) of base oil. For the massage you can use a shallow dish in which to put some oil, or use a small bottle with a stopper. If you are planning to massage frequently, you could prepare a mixture by filling 28 or 54ml (1 or 2fl oz) glass bottles. If you add an optional teaspoon of wheatgerm oil the mixture will be preserved for a longer period.

GETTING READY

After mixing up the oils it is important to make sure you have everything else you need before beginning the massage, so that you can give your full attention to your partner. The surface on which you massage should be comfortable but firm, giving your partner's body full support. You may need towels for warmth, and pillows to raise your partner's body. Have a supply of tissues, some water, and containers for the oil. Check to make sure the containers are well balanced as it is extremely easy to knock them over as you move.

Before giving a massage, it is important also to prepare yourself. Never give a massage if you are tired. The contact between you and your partner becomes so close that your very thoughts can be almost sensed.

In order to relax the spine and release any neck or shoulder tension, follow the simple but effective movements shown over the following few pages. You and your partner can do these exercises together or you can ask your partner to watch you, giving you help through feedback or touch. After the exercises, ask your partner to gently massage your neck and shoulders before you start, so you will have received before you give. Finally, be creative with your room. Turn it into a sensual retreat, filling it with things you enjoy. Make sure it is warm, the lighting is soft, and that you will not be disturbed.

1▲ Before starting a massage it is important to tune into how your partner feels. Take all the time you need to relax together and establish a strong, intimate bond.

15

2▲ When you are ready, try some gentle breathing to relax your mind and body. Lie on your back, knees bent, and place your hands on your abdomen. Simply allow your body to breathe naturally, feeling the rise and fall of your hands.

3▼ After five or ten minutes, let each part of your body relax in turn. Then drawing your knees up to your chest, spread your arms, and slowly lower your left leg, and then your right leg, to the floor on one side. Next do this in reverse. This gives a good stretch but does not strain.

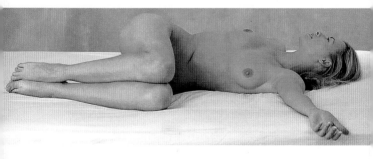

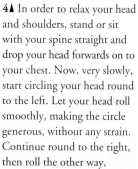

4▲ In order to relax your head and shoulders, stand or sit with your spine straight and drop your head forwards on to your chest. Now, very slowly, start circling your head round to the left. Let your head roll smoothly, making the circle generous, without any strain. Continue round to the right, then roll the other way,

completing the circle at your chest. Raise your head slowly to straighten your spine.

5▲ Roll each shoulder in turn, slowly and evenly, focusing only on that movement.

6▲ To relax the spine, sit on your heels, your forehead on the floor. Now slowly start uncurling your spine, one vertebra at a time, until you reach a sitting position. Your lower back works first, and your head comes last, rolling up evenly through the spine.

7► To ease your neck and shoulders, ask your partner to massage them for you. Your partner's fingers should be

placed over your shoulders, without squeezing, so the thumbs are free to gently knead and press. The thumbs can circle, press and squeeze the muscles, starting a few centimetres out from the spine on either side. From here the movement continues, squeezing and lifting, out along the top of the shoulders. Returning to the spine, your partner should continue the movement downwards, keeping the same position of the hands. As your partner feels knots and tension, he should pay them special attention.

8✔ To relax the neck muscles, you can use some simple self-massage. Hold your hand over the back of your neck, arching in the middle to avoid the spine, with the heel of your hand on one side and your fingertips on the other. Now by raising the arch of your hand, bring your fingertips and heel towards each other, gently working and squeezing the muscles on either side of your spine. With a rhythmic motion, work up your neck muscles to the base of your skull, where a lot of tension collects. Spend some time here and then work back down again. Use a pressure that feels comfortable. Drop your head slightly to open your neck muscles, slowly straightening as you reach the base of your skull.

THE ART OF TOUCHING

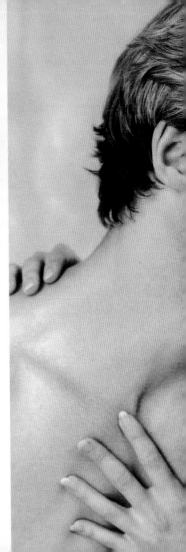

Massage is about touch, and touch is about communication. Thoughts and feelings can be communicated through our hands. How we touch can reflect and alter our partner's feelings and our own, which flow back and forth as our partner responds. The quality of our touch can transform a massage into a beautifully evocative, creative experience. However, no matter how gentle a person's feelings are for their partner, massage involves structured touch, which must be learnt to be accomplished properly.

The Basics

The three basic types of touch, which are used regularly in this book, are effleurage, petrissage and friction. Effleurage is an oiling stroke, good for getting to know your partner's body. Petrissage uses a pumping, kneading motion, which is wonderful for releasing tension. Friction presses into specific problem zones, best used for small areas, gives a feeling of deep release.

Within the range of traditional movements (see pages 23–24), there is a whole world of versatility, literally at your fingertips. For large sweeping movements, being precise, or simply for different sensations, every part of the hand can work to subtle effect. Different parts of the hand can be used to increase pressure, to touch lightly or playfully tease. Try these variations out on your partner, increasing confidence and ability as you experiment. Do not limit your movements to your hands. Use your whole body to increase pleasure in imaginative ways.

Sensual Massage Techniques

Keep the body contact close and sensitive, using rubs and brushes for sensation and delight. A whole body brush is a wonderful experience, while trailing, especially flicking, hair has a pleasurably unexpected feel.

We all instinctively have different ways to touch that convey different messages. Whether we are feeling loving, relaxed, sensual, or playful, we spontaneously express ourselves. The parts of our bodies that we use to express the tenderness of love can be very different from, say, erotic arousal. In a loving massage, we make use of these different nuances, when senses and receptivity are heightened. Like rolling waves, sensual caresses follow strokes for deep relaxation. Erotic arousal becomes dispersed through playful teasing, constantly affirming feelings of love. Sensual massage is an intimate way of expressing your feelings about each other. Like a unique conversation, each massage will be different.

1▼ effleurage This is the first stroke of any massage, and is used to spread the oil, as well as to make contact and explore your partner's body. Starting with your hands flat, fingers relaxed, glide lightly down the body, feeling for knots or tension. Allow your fingers to spread as you sweep round to return, gradually trailing off with the fingertips. Generally, you should increase the pressure as you stroke towards the heart. This stroke relaxes the body, affecting the nerves beneath the skin, and helps return the blood flow to your partner's heart.

2▼ petrissage Here deeper strokes, good for fleshy areas, are used. Kneading is the most useful example. Grasp the flesh, pushing your thumb in and away from you. Use your fingers to roll the flesh back towards you. Like kneading dough, move your hands alternately, with a squeezing, rolling, lifting action. Kneading frees the muscle, increasing circulation.

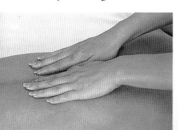
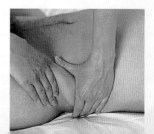

23

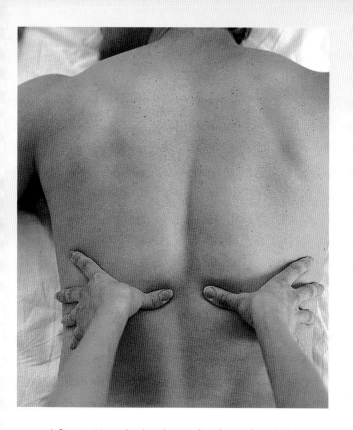

3▲ friction Here, the thumbs are used to apply specific pressure to joints, deep tissue and muscle over bone. Press down using the pads of your thumbs, circling slightly on each spot for deeper penetration. Friction brings release and stimulates your partner's circulation.

4► fingertips The surface of the skin contains billions of nerve endings stimulated by the lightest touch. Using featherlight strokes you can increase its sensitivity. Using the pads of your fingers, lightly trail down your partner's skin. 'Walk' your fingers down his back for light sensations. Gently caress the delicate areas of his face and run your fingers through his hair. When stroking with your fingers, keep your wrists relaxed and flexible and break any contact gently. Brush strokes will make the transition softly from one area of the body to another.

gives a warm sense of contact. You can use it to circle, or put one hand on top of the other, increasing the pressure in the centre. For a slight variation, you can also tilt your hand, increasing the pressure either at the edge or the forefinger joint. This is useful when working round the shoulder blade.

5► flat of hand The flat of the hand can be used for introductory strokes and to 'iron out' across the back, moving outwards from beside the spine. The movement can also be used where stronger pressure is needed, for example, along the thigh. The flat of the hand used softly

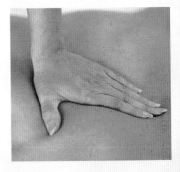

6▼ rolling thumbs As well as using the pads of the thumbs to press, the thumbs can also be used in a rolling movement. Tilting your thumbs very slightly, use the whole length of your thumb to push the muscle away from you. In a rolling movement, one thumb continues where the other stopped. Keep the rolls reasonably short, and by using your thumbs alternately, you create a feeling of one continuous flow. Rolling can be used to work down alongside the spine, on the soles of the feet, palms, or gently down the nose. The fingers can be curled or spread, but press only with the thumbs.

7▼ knuckles Curl your fingers into a fist, with your thumb tucked in or protruding, and bend your wrist over so your knuckles are exposed. Now press down into the flesh, using a circling, twisting motion, being attentive to your partner's pressure needs. The knuckles are only used for fleshy, resistant areas,

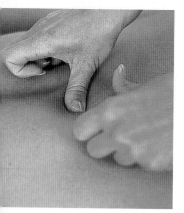

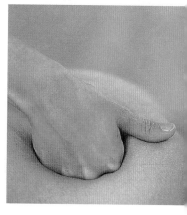

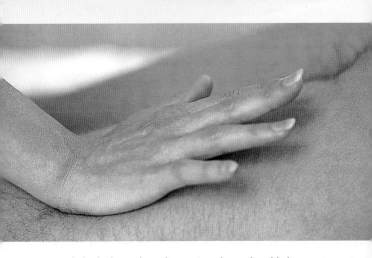

particularly the buttocks and, with care, the soles of the feet. By rippling your fingers as you 'knuckle', an intriguing sensation is produced, altering the intensity of the pressure. Keep your wrist straight while knuckling, as this gives a little more strength to the movement.

8▲ heel Bend your wrist back, lift your palm and fingers slightly and push away from you, along the muscle, with the heel of the hand. This gives the stroke added strength, penetrates the muscle deeply, and gives a satisfying sensation. The heel can be used where added strength is needed, such as the thigh muscles. It is used for deep circling, especially over firm, fleshy areas, like the buttocks. It can also be used to press into muscular areas, while not losing sensitivity from your touch. Keep your elbow slightly bent to create an angle between your shoulder, elbow and wrist.

9▼ tiger's mouth So called to describe the shape of the hands when the thumb and forefinger are spread, this position, also known as a 'V', is used to squeeze along muscles after effleurage. Place your thumb and forefinger on either side, adjusting the angle to fit comfortably around the muscles. Push upwards, away from you, adjusting the angle of your hand to accommodate the muscles' increased bulk. Push as far as you can with a firm pressure, but not too hard, until you reach along the muscles' length. You may prefer to use both hands, one behind the other, to give the movement extra strength.

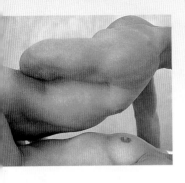

MASSAGE TIPS

• In sensual massage, you can be creative with your body, in keeping contact and in the parts you choose to touch.

• Hair feels particularly good on the body, either sweeping over the skin, or small flicks over hands and feet.

• Full body brushes, with skin touching or tantalizingly close, arouse exciting feelings.

• As you massage, use all the parts of your body for contact, arousing your partner's senses and increasing pleasure for you.

MASTERING THE TOUCH

1▲ the loving touch expresses the tenderness and closeness we feel, the softness the other arouses in us.

2▼ the erotic touch arouses your lover, stimulating both body and sexual fantasy.

3▲ the relaxing touch is calm, soothing, comforting and relieves strain softly with gentle strokes.

4▼ the sensual touch lets us experience feeling our partner through our skin and giving great pleasure.

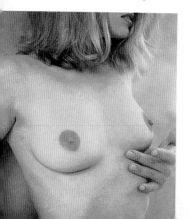

5▲ the stimulating touch
can come as a surprise,
waking and alerting your
partner. An invigorating
touch, it sends pulses
throughout the body. Good
for sharpening the senses, it
gives an instant energy lift.

6▸ the playful touch is just
for fun, to make each other
laugh, to play together and to
let go together. Teasing soon
gets rid of seriousness and is a
great tension release and
natural restorer. Use the ways
you naturally touch your
partner in addition to your
massage strokes. Above all,
bring a sense of playfulness to
the massage, so that it is an
enjoyable experience. As you
approach the massage in an
adventurous spirit, a sense of
fun will be a vital ingredient.
Experiment with touching
and totally give in to pleasure.

31

FULL
SENSUAL
MASSAGE

*Giving your partner a
full sensual body massage
is an extension of the
movements shown in the*
*last section. A sensual
massage incorporates
the strokes traditionally
used for relaxation with
caresses to arouse and
stimulate. While you
relax your partner's
body, you arouse and
heighten the senses
through your movements.
As you use your hands,*

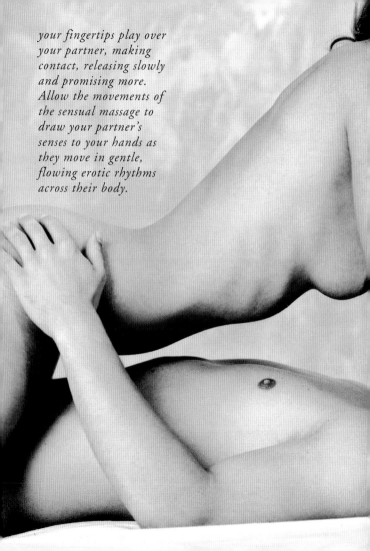

your fingertips play over your partner, making contact, releasing slowly and promising more. Allow the movements of the sensual massage to draw your partner's senses to your hands as they move in gentle, flowing erotic rhythms across their body.

SENSUAL HANDS

The quality of your touch and the way you use your
hands change when you give a sensual massage. It is a
powerful combination: soft, releasing strokes, firm
pressure strokes to penetrate the muscles, together with
light, tantalizing touches. The changes go in cycles, the
movements rhythmic and flowing, blending from one
into the next. To relax your partner use soft, soothing
strokes to explore the body and ease away any immediate
tension. The pressure, while gentle, is definite and firm.
Deep pressure strokes go right into the body, reducing
any build-up of tension in the muscles. The relief of
being touched so deeply is almost tangible. To enhance
your sensual strokes, use a lighter touch that is less
defined, releasing slowly, and lingering as you finish. For
example, after squeezing up a muscle, gently release your
hand, then trail your fingers delicately along the skin. The
final moments of the movement become almost
imperceptible. As you massage, use your hands to build
the excitement for your partner, then through stillness
discharge the feelings you have aroused through the body.

CREATIVE CONTACT

When you give a massage for relaxation, your body
movements are unobtrusive, the focus being the
therapeutic benefits for your partner. As you give a
sensual massage, try to involve your body more and your
enjoyment and whole-heartedness will be communicated
to your partner. Sensual brushes and full skin contact will
enhance your partner's experience, adding to the sensual
pleasure. During massage, pay attention to the nuances of

touch, exploring and making contact creatively. Every
stroke should be a source of pleasure for your partner, so
it is important to listen to the responses of the body. You
will very quickly feel or sense if something is not quite
right. Ask your partner to provide feedback as you go

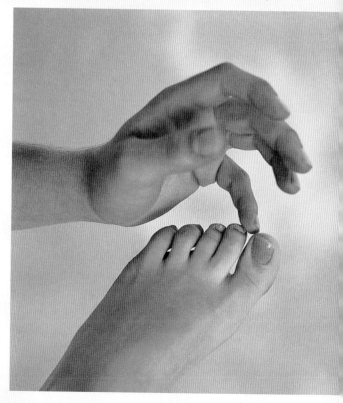

along. Far from detracting from the massage this enhances your communication. The beauty comes when you are so finely tuned to each other that needs and responses are completely automatic. At first you will need to practice a little. While the hands learn surprisingly fast, the most important factor is the flow of feelings from your heart. If you are massaging simply to give to your partner, your partner's body will trust your hands. Trust

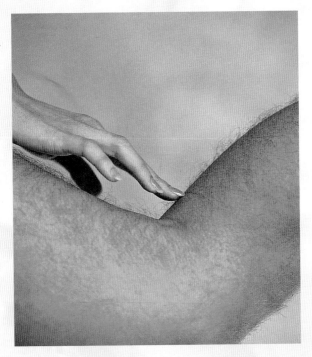

is a vital ingredient of the massage and increases as the experience progresses. As you will discover, there is nothing so deeply erotic. Use the sounds of your breathing, your own unique noises, to please and arouse your partner. There can be nothing more enjoyable for your partner than to know that you are receiving pleasure from giving the massage. This applies equally as you receive. Express your appreciation and satisfaction.

WHERE TO MASSAGE

Through sensual massage, each area of the body is brought to life, in a process of continuing discovery. The soft, inner parts of the body are extremely sensual and erotic. For example, the crook of the elbow, the throat or the back of the knee will all tingle with sensuality when touched. While special areas of the body stimulate more than others, arousing massage makes the whole body an erogenous zone. Take time to explore, deriving pleasure from each new discovery. Use the process of the massage to create and be inventive, developing the eroticism of the body. Touching sensually and sensitively, you can electrify your partner, increasing the intensity between you.

In the following pages you have a step-by-step guide to a full, flowing sensual massage. Each stage and movement follows on from the next, covering both the back and the front of the body. Use the sequence to guide you, adding your own experience and ideas, and of course your own unique knowledge of your partner. Also included is more general information to give you further insights into the body and more especially into your partner. Everything is there simply to be used. Enjoy bringing the strokes to life.

THE BACK

The back is a wonderful area to massage. Rich with nerves and powerful muscles, more than any other area it cries out to be touched. By massaging the back the whole body is affected, renewing that vital connection with ourselves. Massaging the back is an extremely effective way to begin the full sensual massage. Once it is relaxed and aroused, the whole body responds.

PREPARING FOR THE MASSAGE
With a sensual massage, the important opening steps set the tone for everything that follows. The first contact speaks volumes. Be totally receptive to your partner, her mood, stillness or inner vibrancy. Sense the feelings of anticipation increase. Be totally willing to give. At the same time, as your hands caress and feel out the body in the first effleurage, note the sensations your partner's skin produces in your hands. Feel the texture, any changes in roughness or smoothness, look at the colour, the elasticity and the warmth. Pay attention to your own feelings as you massage in the oil, allowing your hands to flow over the skin. Allow the invitation of your partner's skin to draw your hands into contact with the back.

USING PRESSURE
The back is a large and variable area to massage and you will need to keep in mind that the kind of

pressure on the shoulders, lower back and buttocks needs to be different. You may find quite a lot of tension in the shoulders, especially in the trapezius muscle that runs across the shoulders, neck and upper back. Pressure here should be sensitive and only slightly firm. With tight muscles it is tempting to use hard pressure but if you press too hard the muscles will fight back.

Once you have massaged the shoulders, move down to the lower back. Exploring the area, glide over the soft contours of the sacrum, buttocks and hips. The lower back can be a particularly vulnerable or strained area, and tightness here can cut off full sensations.

Deep pressure around the buttocks feels satisfying and will release strong erotic feelings in your partner. Follow deep relaxation round the hips by muscle stimulation, then soft skin caresses to bring the senses to life. Relaxation followed by caresses and arousal provide a combination difficult to resist.

THE SENSITIVE ZONES
When you come to massaging the spine and neck, be particularly careful. Both areas are very sensitive and require a more gentle pressure. Keeping 2.5cm (1 inch)

out from the spine, press evenly along the muscle bands, paying attention where you feel raised areas of muscle. Use your fingers to feel the texture and tightness, and as you press correspond your

39

movements to your partner's exhalation. As nerves branch out from the spine connecting to the whole body, this will be a highly sensitive and releasing movement for your partner. As you reach the top of the neck, bring your hands once more to your partner's lower back to draw awareness away from the head, and fully connect the back. This movement is a reminder of the feelings aroused earlier, as gentle sensations diffuse through the body. You need to change position several times during this massage so give yourself room to manoeuvre.

BODY AWARENESS

The way we seem to see things means that we tend to divide them into parts. But the reality is that each area of the body opens into another and that every part is connected to the next. For example, the powerful shoulders are needed for arm movement, the legs are affected by the lower back. The lower back leads into the swell of the buttocks, the ribs follow round to the swell of the breasts. Simply open your mind as your fingers explore. With each stroke, a whole new world opens up, every inch of skin has something different to reveal.

The skin is the largest organ of the body. Sensory receptors lie just below its surface, relaying messages to the central nervous system. These receptors can be stimulated by extremely light pressure. Some respond to a firm pressure, while others alert the body to pain. As you massage, a lighter pressure will generally arouse and stimulate, while a heavier pressure will relax and release the body. Use variations of pressure for the sensual massage, arousing, releasing then arousing again.

BACK INJURIES

While injuries should receive medical attention, you can ease problems as you massage. Do not massage directly over an injury, but work the surrounding area gently. Muscles around an injury often go into spasm to protect it. Massage can help relieve the stiffness caused by this, allowing the injury to heal. The body will often compensate to protect a painful area, so when the right shoulder hurts, you should also work the left shoulder. If the problem is caused by tension, work on and around the shoulder, easing the muscles outwards from the spine. Start lightly, then move in deeper, spreading and moving the shoulder frequently. For problems in the shoulders always include the lower back. For neck problems massage the upper back first, then work on the neck from underneath. For the lower back, ease with sacral circling, then massage the buttocks and middle back, spreading outwards from the spine.

1► Before you begin the massage, kneel at your partner's head and gently stroke the hair away from her face. Rest your fingers softly on the back of the head and neck before beginning the massage. Let your fingertips sense your partner, at the same time as your own feelings begin to flow out through your hands.

2► Apply a little oil to your hands, then begin to effleurage your partner's back. As you sweep down the back, be aware of the muscle curves, the colour and texture of the skin. Allow your hands to fan and undulate over your partner's body, applying only very light pressure as you pass over its contours.

3► Glide down towards your partner's lower back, moving over the hips and buttocks with your fingertips. Then spread your hands to come up the back once more, dragging

and squeezing slightly over ribs and shoulder blades. Repeat the stroke several times to cover the entire back, easing away tension from the whole area and bringing the skin alive.

4▲ As you end the movement, gently draw your hands up the back and neck and through your partner's hair, stroking through with your fingertips right to the very ends of the hair.

5 ◄ After you have effleuraged the whole back, you gently knead the top of one shoulder with your thumbs, squeezing the little rolls of flesh with your fingertips. Beginning at the outer edge, continue the movement to the neck, ending with longer teasing squeezes to draw your partner's senses. You should always work on the shoulder facing away from you, where the muscle is exposed. As you knead the shoulder, also brush the arms or knead the neck, play with your partner's senses, varying the intensity of your touch.

6 ◄ After the kneading motion, press your thumb in along the muscle, making small half-circling movements from the edge of the shoulder inwards. Press firmly to begin the circle, easing the pressure as the thumb moves round. Draw your thumb away from each circle lightly and slowly.

This continues the easing effect that you began with the kneading. After easing, let the pressure trail away, continuing contact and arousal with your fingertips. Gently easing the muscles is much more effective than using hard pressure.

7▼ Move to your partner's side after completing the thumb rolls from the fleshy shoulder triangle to the spine. Stroke down the muscles to the side of the spine with the whole of your hand, using light, caressing movements. Alternating your hands, trail lightly with your fingertips as you complete each stroke, lingering over the skin. Draw down, using these rolling brushstrokes, from the neck all the way down to the base of the spine.

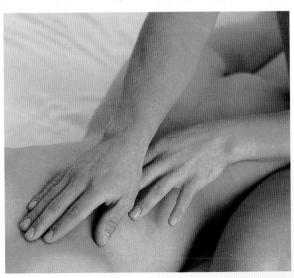

8 ◄ To complete your massage of the upper back, move your partner's arm behind her back, easing the muscle around the shoulder blade. Still with your lower hand supporting her shoulder, use the heel of your hand to push the muscles on the blade itself. Move your hand diagonally towards the shoulder joint, pushing slowly and deeply along the muscles. Ease the pressure to follow the contour of the shoulder down the arm.

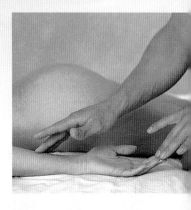

Knead once again, then repeat movements 5–9 on the other side of the body.

9 ✓ Bringing the arm back to your partner's side, use light brushstrokes all the way down the arm to the fingertips. Brush slowly and sensually until, fingertip to fingertip, you continue the sensation even after your hand has gone.

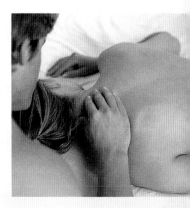

10 ► Gently knead your partner's neck, using slow, gentle strokes to tease out any tension, then hold the hair softly as she turns her head.

11▲ Moving to your partner's legs, pour a little more oil into your hands. Now begin to effleurage the buttocks. Fan and spread your fingers, following the body contours, around the lower back, hips and the tops of the thighs. Sweep your hands upwards and outwards, shaped to the curves of flesh, until every bit is covered with oil.

12► With your hands pressing downwards and inwards, circle the heels of your hands into the buttocks, moving down, upwards and out to loosen the muscles.

13► Circle your thumbs on either side of the spine (2.5cm/1in away from the spine itself) of the lower back, then spread your hands out across the back. As you move the hands apart, feel the dimples and curves of the buttocks, ending the movement with your hands curved around the hips.

14► Moving across to the side, knead your partner's buttocks with a satisfying, generous movement. Then press in with the heel of your hand, making deep, circling movements, bringing the pressure in towards you. Feel the muscles, and press around the hips, ease out any tensions bringing the area to life.

15► Continue this movement with your fingertips, gradually easing into the hip joint to send wonderful sensations of deep release through your partner's pelvis and thighs.

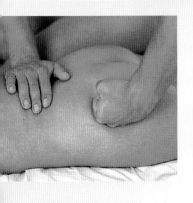

loosen tension. Press into the flesh, feeling how the buttocks respond under your touch, encouraging the muscles to release and open.

17▶ Plucking is a light-hearted and stimulating movement that pulls the flesh away from the body. Keeping your wrists relaxed, pull mounds of flesh between your fingers and thumbs up towards you. Alternate your hands to make quick, light, plucking movements, enjoying the rippling of your partner's flesh. This playful movement will stimulate and arouse your partner, spreading tingling or tickling sensations all across the buttocks and right up the back.

16▲ Knuckling completes the deep pressure movements. Form your hand into a fist, pressing firmly yet sensitively with your knuckles. As your hands are now familiar with the area, you will be able to

18▶◀ Now that the buttocks are alive and tingling, stroke up very, very lightly between them with the backs of your hands. Watch your partner's skin thrill to

the touch as you continue. As the sensations heighten, use a spreading stroke to diffuse the erotic feelings away.

19▼ Cup your hands over the sacrum, then slowly pull your hands apart, hugging them over the hips and bringing them down the thighs. This diffusion is completed as you trail off with your fingertips as you finish the stroke.

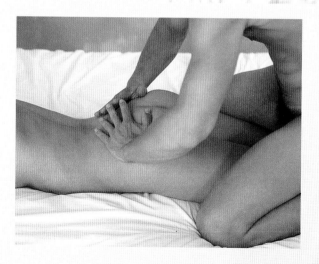

20 Move your position so that you can reach the entire back easily, in preparation for the 'ironing' stroke. Starting the movement just above the hips, position your hands either side of the spine. The heels of your hands face inwards, fingertips spreading out across the back. Then start to draw your hands apart, using a firm, even pressure, to slide your fingers around the ribs. With the whole of the flat of the hand, iron out the muscles as you push away from the spine, dispersing tension in the dorsal muscles, the broad muscles that help move the arms. As your heels move towards your partner's sides, add light caressing touches with your fingers to the feelings of stretch and release. Then with your fingertips, drag back towards the spine, bringing the heels of your hands back together. Position your hands for the next stroke slightly farther up the back, and with no break in continuity, repeat the stroke. Work leisurely up the back. Keep the pressure on the outward strokes, your movements big and generous, which your partner will enjoy.

21 As you come to the upper back, hook your hands around her shoulders, pulling very slightly up and back towards you.

22▌ To continue the movement, slide your hands evenly from around the shoulders, and bring them, palms flat, towards each other. Lead with your fingers so your arms cross over each other, the hands hugging the body on opposite sides.

23◣ Curling your fingers to the form of the body, pull your hands back towards each other, until they cross in the centre of the back. Continue the pressure movement as your hands slide apart from each other, moving to mold round the ribs on either side. This movement has a hugging, wringing feel, and is extremely satisfying, as first the muscles are moved in

towards the spine, then slowly smoothed and stretched away. Without breaking the rhythm, use your fingertips to caress your partner's sides. As you turn your hands, point your fingers up the body. Then drag your fingers as you bring the hands back towards each other, cross over, and slide once more to the position on opposite sides. Moving slightly farther down the back, repeat the wringing and returning until once again you are at the hips. Keeping the movement continuous, snaking down your partner's back, will arouse delightful feelings.

the spine. (Never massage directly over the spine.) Start to move your thumbs gently up the muscles, avoiding pressure, then press in where you feel tension or the muscles rise. You can use the thumbs very sensitively, keeping the pressure and withdrawal steady. Releasing tension, this sparks sensations through the whole body.

24▲ From your position at the lower back, place your thumb pads on the bands of muscle running either side of

25▶ Having continued the pressure movements up either side of the spine, you need to change the pressure for the neck. As it will be turned, and is also extremely sensitive, a much softer movement is required. Use thumb and forefinger to press either side of the neck, reaching up to the very base of the skull. Releasing tension, this produces dreamy feelings.

26▶ Leaving one hand at the neck, rest the other on the lower back to connect the sensation down the spine.

BE CREATIVE

After following the structured massage sequence, why not spend some time being creative with your lover's back in other ways. It feels good to simply enjoy your partner's back and feel her pleasure vibrating through the skin.

• Bring your body close to hers, and envelop her with a full body slide. The whole body contact feels great, and the fact that you can't get away from her back feels even better – for both of you! After the intensity of the massage, it feels good to relax together, be playful, inventive and enjoy each other to the full.

• In a slightly more reflective mood, trace out every detail of your partner's back with small caresses. Her back, and the way you have come to know it, will surprise you. In massage, you come very close to your partner. Follow your instincts and if this is a good time to pause for a moment, be quiet together, and let your feelings merge. The softest moments and the smallest movements can often be the most intimate. Your lover's soft body curves provide a wonderful place to rest.

• Blowing on the skin feels sensational. After the warm pressure of your hands during massage, the light, cool touch of your breath provides a beautiful contrast on the skin. Blow along the length of your partner's back and around the lower back curves. Bring your lips very close so the breath feels warmer, and watch the way the surface of the skin responds. Holding your partner continues the closeness of your contact, and enables you to brush her body with even more of your skin.

• Try tracing gentle curves over your partner's skin with the backs of your hands. Idly stroke her over her whole body, in soft circles and curves, without stopping the rhythm of your hands. These gentle caresses will feel very loving and warming.

Taking time to appreciate and admire your partner, seeing and feeling the difference as your massage progresses, the intimacy of the contact is such that there is almost no difference between you; your partner's body feels as familiar as your own. As for your partner, time loses all meaning in the bliss of endless variations of touch and delightful sensations.

THE BACKS OF THE LEGS

It is a natural progression of the sensual massage to now move your eyes down your partner's body to the legs. Notice their power, their length, the way they spread and the form of their muscles. Follow the contours around the thighs and buttocks, and the change in skin texture coming down to the feet. As the calves taper towards the ankles, place your hands softly around the heels.

Of all the areas of the body, the legs often suffer the most neglect, but are fully deserving of attention as they lead us forward towards new experiences.

LEG MASSAGE

When you effleurage the backs of the legs you move from your partner's ankles up the calves to the thighs. Take care when you reach the backs of the knee as they are very sensitive. So too is the inner thigh. Only gentle pressure should be used in these areas. You should brush only lightly if your partner has raised veins. Your partner will love the leg stretches, but do not bend past the point of resistance. After massaging the legs, the movements for passive exercise will help to stretch and tone the muscles and loosen the joints. Always aim for the optimum movement within your partner's range. Lowering your legs slowly and gently draws out exquisite feelings of release.

ABOUT THE LEGS

The legs not only contain the longest bone in the body, the femur, but also one of its most complicated joints, the knee. The sciatic nerve, the body's largest peripheral nerve, passes down through the pelvis and back of the leg to the foot. Usually, any pain in this nerve has a connection in the lower back. The leg muscles are particularly powerful, with three long muscles (the hamstrings) running down the backs of the thighs. The feet provide both mobility and stable support, but it is the bones of the leg that directly bear the body's weight. The legs are extremely powerful and highly sensitive. The backs and sides of the thigh are responsive to firm pressure, while the inner thigh and buttocks are more delicate. The feelings aroused here can be very erotic. The calf muscles enjoy reasonably firm touch, but for a woman, it may need to be quite light. Check with your partner. The feet and ankles delight in massage and movement, enjoying the unaccustomed freedom it brings.

HEAD TO TOE AWARENESS
Completing the massage at the feet gives immediate satisfaction. As reflex zones of the feet relate to all the organs of the body, massage here can revitalize the whole system and seems to penetrate the very bones. At the end of the massage, pause to rest and to allow the sensations flooding over your partner's body to diffuse gently away.

Massaging the back of the body provides strength and support for the vulnerable front. With the entire back of the body relaxed and alive with sensation, finish off with gentle brushstrokes to bring awareness from head to toe.

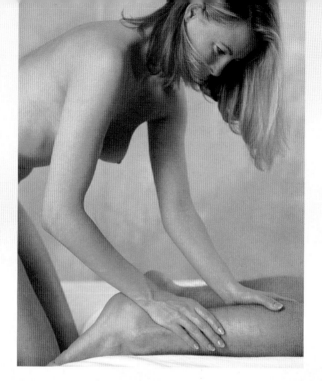

1▲ Apply some more oil to your hands and kneel at your partner's feet. Then begin to effleurage one leg, starting at the ankle.

2►◄ Sweep up the leg to cover the back of the thigh

and the buttock. You can effleurage the legs one at a time, or both at once, depending on your reach and balance. With the pressure on the upward stroke, keep the movement as one long sweep, allowing your hands to follow the curve and spread of your partner's muscles. Include the buttocks and hips as you stroke, as well as the sensitive, easily aroused inner thigh. Returning on the downward stroke, drag slightly with your fingertips around the back of the knee and calf, following the shape of the calf muscles. Tapering down with your fingers along the tendon to the heel, sweep around the feet and then return upwards to repeat the stroke. Apply a little bit more oil on your hands so that they glide easily over the legs.

3► Returning to your partner's feet, form your hand into the tiger's mouth (see page 28), clasping the leg just above the ankle. With thumb and forefinger spread on either side, squeeze up the muscles as they swell to form the calf. Widen your hand as the muscles broaden, releasing the pressure as you near the knee. Squeezing

movements like this help to remove toxins, in particular lactic acid. The build-up of toxins will be greater in well-formed muscles, so if this is the case, use both hands.

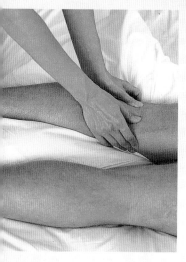

4◄ This is a wonderfully sensitive area that deserves special attention. Place the length of your thumbs in the centre of the crease of your partner's knee. Keeping the pressure slight, slowly draw your thumbs apart. As your thumbs reach around the joint, lightly and slowly circle, dipping downwards, then sweeping up through the natural dimples. End the stroke with your thumbs trailing off up the back of your partner's thigh.

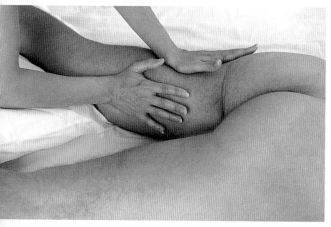

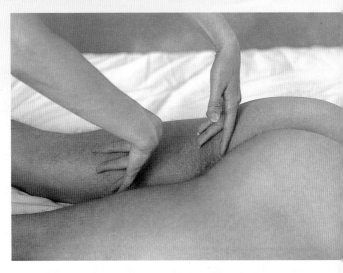

5 ◄ To perform this, you may need to adjust your position, moving up to your partner's thigh. Use the flat of your hands to press firmly up the muscles, keeping the pressure light on the sensitive inner thigh. If the leg muscles are particularly strong, use the heels of your hands to press up the back and the outer thigh. Continue pressure towards the buttock, moving across and over the hip.

6▲ With the backs of your fingers, stroke up along the thighs toward the buttocks. As the backs of the fingers are very sensitive, this movement will also be enjoyable for you. Keep the pressure light enough to sensitize and arouse, but for a man especially, not soft enough to tickle. End the strokes curling over the buttocks, sending sensations right up your partner's spine.

7▲ With broad, deep, enthusiastic strokes, begin kneading the back of your partner's thigh. Keep the pressure at the back and side, working only lightly over the inner area where the leg artery runs. Twist and roll the flesh to loosen up the muscles, freeing the thigh for sensations that run right down to the feet. Stroking gently back down the leg, place one hand over the heel and one around the front of your partner's foot.

8◄ Then lifting the leg slightly, pull back towards you, giving a stretch that can be felt in the lower back and hips.

9▼ Raise the leg and begin to circle it slowly, several times in one direction, then several times in the other direction. Take the whole leg weight, holding the foot and ankle for support, and only circle it

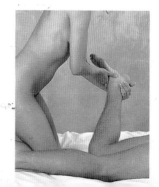

well within your partner's range. Felt in the hip and knee, this movement gives a satisfying roll to the muscles at the back of the thigh.

10▼ For a final releasing stretch along the front of the thigh, press the leg back, aiming the heel towards the buttock. Applying pressure gradually through the arms, press until you feel the leg resist. Then lower it gently, while maintaining contact with your hands.

11 ◄ Complete the leg by bringing it back towards you and begin to work deeply around the ankle joint. Using your thumbs, circle slowly and evenly on both sides, working close to the bone. Now, move down to the foot. Support it from underneath with your thumbs.

12 ◄ Interlace your fingers across the sole, then slowly start to draw them apart. This action spreads the foot, leading to a sense of freedom and expansion. Ease the pressure as you reach the sides of the foot, cupping your hands around the instep and ankle joint. Do this movement several times over.

13 ◄ Lowering the leg to rest on your thigh as a support, press over the sole of the foot with your thumbs. Using a reasonably firm pressure, press with the pads to cover the entire foot. This creates a wonderfully releasing

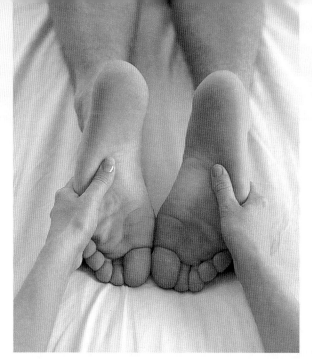

movement, which reaches down the entire body. Keep the pressure and withdrawal slow and steady, to increase the hypnotic rhythm and sheer delight of the movement. Then place the foot down gently, and start the entire sequence on the other leg.

14▲ While your partner's body pulses with exquisite sensations, close the back of the leg massage by resting for a moment or so, while you hold your partner's feet firmly but gently in your hands. This time of stillness is beneficial to both of you.

HAVE FUN

The legs feel and look wonderful when they are relaxed and supple. After the leg massage, take some time to explore a variety of sensations and sensual movements with your partner.

The soles of the feet are very sensitive, and can often be ticklish, but they are extremely responsive to touch. Play with your partner's toes: they can be very erogenous. They can also be a source of great pleasure and childish laughter.

• For an interesting sensual feel, try stimulating your partner's feet with your hair. Brush softly with your hair all over the foot, or, if your partner can take it and your hair is long enough, flick the ends at the soles of his feet. Short, sharp flicks can be very arousing. It also feels good to your partner to lose his foot amongst your hair!

• Leg movement can be very graceful. Leg to leg, sole to sole, brings the legs together, concentrating feeling and contact through the feet. Use the sensitivity of your feet to feel each other, experimenting with the different shapes your legs create. For playful movement, you can bicycle the legs together, pushing and stretching to feel the angle of your limbs. Feel the sensations you produce as you press and move against one another, using the soft, sensitive pads of your feet.

• Take time getting to know your partner's legs intimately. Brush against them with your entire body, or softly caress them with your toes. Slowly feel their entire length with your feet. Gently blowing between the toes feels very sensual, separating each one and giving a little pull. Rub your legs, hip to hip or back to back, feeling every detail of your partner's skin.

• The natural result of massaging is that the body becomes more integrated, a complete whole once again. Movements are spontaneous and expressive; it is almost as if you have become re-acquainted with your limbs. Moving the legs when they feel connected to the back, is completely effortless. Express the pleasure with your partner, sharing the enjoyment. Get to know your partner's body through your legs, keeping the contact intimate and special.

THE NECK

With your partner lying on her back, position yourself at her head, with your knees on either side. Before you start, take a moment to be sensitive to your partner's body. The front of the body is naturally more vulnerable and open than the back, and your massage should reflect this. See the soft, relaxed roundness in the way the body lies, from the swell of the breasts to the abdomen, hips and legs. Note the delicate facial features, the muscles of the neck and then concentrate your full attention on the shoulders and gently bring your hands towards your partner's chest.

RELEASING TENSION

The neck often carries a lot of tension, so in this position the muscles are resting naturally, without having to support the head. A soft, releasing massage on the neck muscles immediately affects the upper back. The most important muscles for neck massage are the trapezius (at

the back of the neck), and the sternolcleidomastoid
(at the side), which turns the head. The cervical vertebrae
supporting the head form a natural spinal curve. If the
neck is lengthened through stretching, a feeling of
release reverberates down the spine.

The sweeping effleurage strokes you use around the
breasts and ribs will connect sensations from the torso to
the neck. In fact as you stretch the neck and push the
shoulders, the whole upper torso begins to release.

To massage the neck, bring your hands to the back of
the neck and use small circles to release. Pressing slowly at
the base of the neck releases tension, at the same time
increasing sensuality. To end the massage, relax the scalp
and tousle your partner's hair, tugging gently at the roots.

It is only after releasing the neck that we feel a
wonderful sense of freedom, the body almost flooding
with euphoria. It is no exaggeration to say that a soft,
relaxed neck creates a softer and more open state of mind.

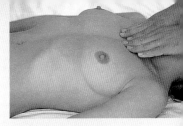

1► Rub more oil on to your fingers. Begin the effleurage by placing your fingertips lightly on the uppermost part of your partner's chest, then sweep the fingers down with your hands between her breasts.

2► Spread your hands out either side of the breastbone to follow the curve of your partner's body, sweeping your fingers round the ribs.

3► As you turn your hands under your partner's breasts, press the flesh firmly, then slowly pull up the side of the body. Drag slightly with your fingertips.

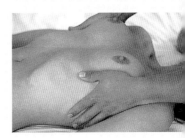

4◄ Curve your hands to dip around the shoulders, then sliding round behind the shoulders, stretch down and away from you with the heels of your hands. Continue by sweeping up the back of the neck, until your fingers are under the base of the skull.

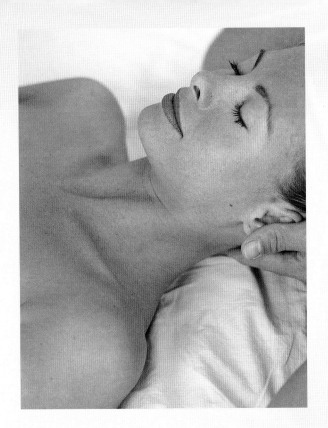

5▲ Complete the movement by stretching up and back towards you, lengthening the neck and releasing tension in the spine. Pull off through the hair and gently lower the head. Complete this movement several times, using luxurious, gliding strokes as you work.

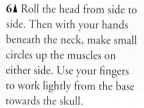

6 Roll the head from side to side. Then with your hands beneath the neck, make small circles up the muscles on either side. Use your fingers to work lightly from the base towards the skull.

7 Turn the head, and after pushing the shoulder down, smooth up the neck with the flat of your hand.

8 As you reach the base of the skull, press in and under with your fingertips, keeping the pressure slow and even.

9 Tousle and 'shampoo' your partner's hair.

10 Finally, finger up to the ends of the hair with your fingertips.

74

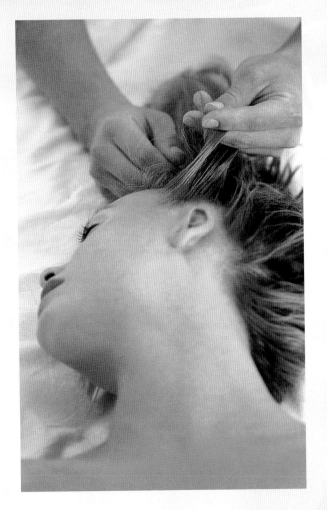

AROUSING THE SENSES

The neck and throat areas are extremely delicate and sensitive. This makes them extremely responsive to touch. Using a tender, delicate stroke will fully open up your partner's senses.

• With the sensitive backs of your fingertips, trace lightly up your partner's throat. Follow every detail, softly drawing up and under the chin. As your touch continues almost imperceptibly, the body will be awash with sensation.

• Alternatively you can gently brush with your forefinger around the crescent of the ear. The skin behind the ear is very soft and delicate. Stimulate it with the pads of your fingers, playing softly along the line of the hair.

• More wonderful sensations are produced by you brushing up the side of her neck with your fingers. Start stroking in the sensitive hollow above the collar bone, and pull softly upwards

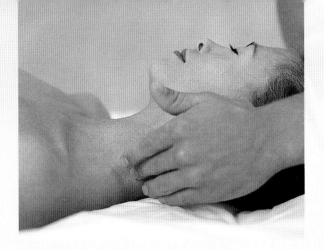

until you reach the dimple behind the ear. This will
send tingles all over the skin, down the spine and around
the scalp. Watch to see the goose bumps on your
partner's flesh as they appear. Choose a few strands of
hair from the highly sensitive nape of your partner's neck,
then gently tease and pull the hairs, keeping them taut
between your fingers. Draw out the sensation by
pulling the very ends.

• Exploring your partner's body and watching closely
the way she responds, increases the feeling between you
of tenderness and intimacy. It is a whole new pleasure to
find ways to please your partner, providing different
sensations for her to experience. As you touch your
partner's body share your experiences – how her body
feels to you and how your touch feels to her.

THE FACE

After the neck and scalp have been massaged and are tingling, turn your attention to the face. By gently massaging the face, you can send glowing feelings all through your partner's head. Beginning at the forehead, rest your hands for a moment, and tune into your partner's state of mind.

The delicate muscles of the face are constantly used to reflect the way we feel, but they can become quite tight. Tension over the forehead, around the eyes, and especially round the jaw prohibits fluidity of facial expression. The mouth, a highly mobile structure, is very sensual, and the nerve endings are extremely sensitive to touch. The forehead, when we feel calm, is relaxed and smooth. Our eyes tell the world how we feel.

THE LOVING TOUCH

It is only when someone actually massages the face that we become aware of how much the muscles are used. As you smooth across your partner's forehead, any tightness will start to diffuse, the feeling spreading as you work around the eyes. Smoothing over the cheeks and around the chin restores feeling and flexibility, completed by broad circling movements to release the jaw. The jaw, which can become clenched tightly, should hang just slightly open, with the tongue relaxed at the bottom of the mouth. By now your partner's face will feel blissfully released – the experience reaches too deep to even talk.

Complete the massage with loving touches to your partner's features, stroking down the nose and tracing lightly with your fingertips around the mouth. Gentle squeezing and pulling of the earlobes can feel wonderful.

1► Smooth a little oil over your fingers. Then place the length of your thumbs in the centre of your partner's forehead, your hands cupped gently around the head. Draw your thumbs apart, gradually and evenly, releasing the pressure as you curve round to the temples.

2► Dipping your thumbs to circle round the temples, bring the movement back, and draw out your thumbs across the eyebrows.

3◄ Without breaking the continuity, place the pads of your thumbs just below the eye-socket ridge. Start from the outer edge, then press gently along the muscles, using tiny movements at even intervals round to the nose.

4▲ Moving your thumbs to rest across the cheekbones, smooth your hands over the cheeks and pull them up towards the ears. Cup your hands gently around the face and spread the muscles upwards into a smile.

81

5► Interlace your fingers under the chin, then pull them apart, spreading up the line of the jaw. Keeping your thumbs above and your forefingers below the jaw line, slide round and upwards until you reach the joint.

6► To release any tightness in the area, ask your partner to slightly drop his jaw, then make slow, broad circles with your fingertips.

7► Softly brush your thumb along the length of your partner's nose, using rolling strokes from the bridge to the very tip.

8◄ Repeat this several times, following the curve to reach his lips. Trace lightly with your fingertips around your partner's mouth.

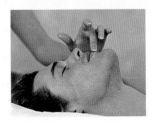

9▲ To continue the stimulation of your partner's senses, squeeze and tug the earlobes between your forefinger and thumb. Slide your whole body down towards the lobes, brushing them with your lips.

THE ARMS

By now relaxation and sensual pleasure will be seeping down your partner's body. You need to move to his side to begin massage on the arms. Look for a moment to absorb each area in detail, following from the shoulder to the slimness of the wrists. Note the way your partner rests his forearm, then bring your eyes to the powerful, sensitive hands. Make soft initial contact at the wrist, then begin the sweep of effleurage strokes up the arms.

When you massage the arms, bear in mind that, like the legs, you can do each part of the massage alternating between the two arms or you can massage one at a time. When you begin work on the inner arm, be aware of the exquisitely sensitive skin on the inner elbow. Take a few moments to sense out the area with your fingertips, stimulating and arousing as you stroke. The movements on the arm should flow into one another, progressing rhythmically up towards the shoulder.

Firm pressure along the upper arm releases the bulk of the muscles, which often become tight and solid. Use the flat of your hand to press and smooth around the armpit, keeping the pressure sensitive yet firm as you explore the dips and curves. Circling movements, followed by slowly releasing the pressure, can have a delightfully erotic feel. A full stretch of your partner's arm is wonderfully releasing, both freeing the arm and having an effect right down the spine. The feeling of someone else stretching your limbs is an unusual, extremely pleasurable experience. As you press down the forearm, moving to the wrist, be aware of the delicate structure. As you circle very gently with your fingertips you can feel the minute detail of the bones.

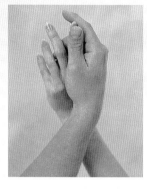

CARESSING THE HANDS
The hands deserve a good deal of attention, being used, almost unconsciously, every second of the day. Without realizing it a lot of tension can build here, only coming to a person's attention when they are receiving a massage on the hands. Spend time caressing and releasing every inch of your partner's fingers, then, after brushstrokes, tenderly entwine them in your own. Just allow the fingers to idly touch and play as a sweet, loving gesture of affection.

ABOUT THE ARMS
Our arms play an important part in our self-expression, as well as being indispensable for work. It is with our arms that we draw people and objects closer, and equally use them to push those things away. We naturally use our arms for our protection, while our hands demonstrate what we say and express the way we feel. We use our hands to manipulate objects, make things or be creative. We hold out our hands to invite contact with another person, and of course, we use our hands for touch. The fingertips are extremely sensitive, and pick up numerous messages that tell us about the world. The palms of the

hands, also very sensitive, are one of the areas from where we issue strength.

The bones of the forearm are so arranged that in order for the arm to turn, one bone rotates around the other. Pressure between the bones can feel extremely good. The wrist provides a fulcrum for movement of the hands, which is facilitated by the structure of the finger joints. Passive movement of these joints always feels good. The nerves supplying the arms start in the neck, so massage around the neck and shoulders often travels down the arms. The biceps and triceps are the strong arm muscles, effecting the movements of the forearm. Interacting with the upper arm, muscles in the back and upper chest facilitate movement of the mobile shoulder joint.

Arm movements are an extension of the body and, flowing and expansive, come from around the shoulders. If the chest is also relaxed and open, this releases energy down the arms. The arm position and movements are

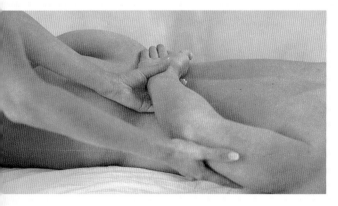

affected if the chest feels tight and held in. When the arms are free, they feel more sensitive and much lighter.

PREVENTING TENSION IN THE ARMS

As you are massaging your partner's arms, note any differences you feel between the left and the right. For people who are right-handed, for example, the right side will tend to be more developed and probably more tense. The right side of the body is primarily controlled by the rational and logical left side of the brain, while the creative, intuitive right side of the brain influences the left side of the body. Very often tension in the arms and shoulders relates to the ways we use our minds. It is important to keep an even balance between activities, and to use both sides of the body. For example, if you are right-handed, keep your left side active. Try and do things with both hands. As a general rule, after muscles have been working, give them a little time to relax.

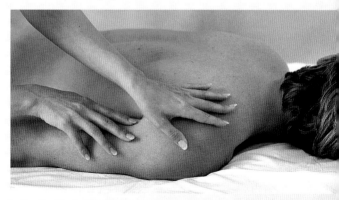

sliding and turning on the lighter downward stroke. Do this movement several times.

2➤ Then, lifting the arm at the wrist, squeeze up the forearm muscles with the tiger's mouth (see page 28). Use the forefinger joint and thumb for extra pressure.

3➤ Work the length of the muscles right up to the elbow, squeezing as you release the pressure to work round the elbow joint. As you press, you will be giving your partner a feeling of deep release, sending wonderful tingling sensations down the whole length of the arms. Press sensitively with your thumb, and feel around the bones, trailing off with small circling movements at the back of the upper arm. As you perform this movement, be careful of the ulnar nerve, situated at the back of the elbow and often known as the funny bone.

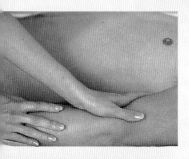

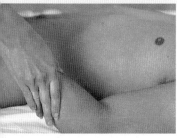

1▲ Apply some oil to your hands, then use effleurage strokes in full gliding movements up the arm. Be sure to oil right up over the shoulder. Gently rock the arm between your hands as you return to loosen any tension. You should only use pressure on the upward stroke. Keep the strokes flowing, free and generous

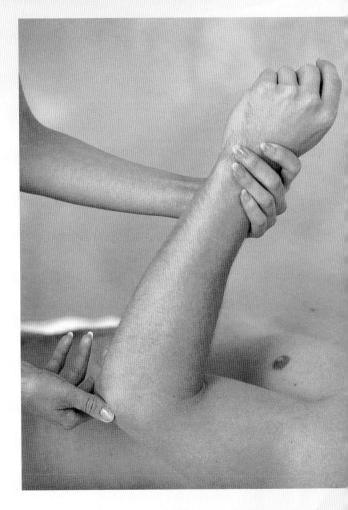

4► Lower your partner's forearm once again, then turn the palm over, supporting the forearm at the wrist. With the flat of your hand, begin smoothing up the inner arm muscles, pressing with reasonable firmness towards the elbow. Sweep round the arm to the wrist as you return and, without breaking the rhythm of your hands, slide up the arm again, exerting some pressure. This will feel both soothing and sensual to your partner and

produces a delightful tingling in his palm. Repeat these strokes several times.

5◄ Afterwards, turn your attention to the inner elbow, and use your fingertips to brush along the crease. This is a very sensitive area and feels wonderful as you stroke along the line of the elbow joint. Use your fingers to stimulate or, dragging along the crease, dip and circle them along the outer edge. Spend several moments here. As you linger over the skin, this will totally mesmerize your partner.

6► Now lift your partner's arm to place it at a right angle across the body, and give the forearm support by holding it at the wrist. Then cup your other hand around the upper arm muscles, and press firmly down toward the shoulder. Squeeze the muscles tightly, using pressure between your heel and fingers. Apply the movement to both outer and inner arm muscles, using your thumbs for extra strength. As you reach the shoulder, slide your hand around the joint. Then supporting the upper arm with both hands, lower it behind your partner's head.

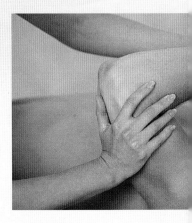

7► Using the flat of your hand, press lightly round the armpit. This movement feels deliciously sensual. If your partner is ticklish, start lightly but firmly, and then increase the pressure. Press and circle using different points of your hands, ending by soft brushstrokes up the arm towards the elbow.

8▲ Positioning yourself behind your partner's head, bend forwards to take hold of his arm.

9►◀ With one hand around his hand and the other supporting the elbow (or you can grip your partner's arm), gently pull the length of the arm back towards you. Start the stretch slowly, increasing the pull until you feel resistance, then ease the pressure. Your partner will feel the stretch around the ribs and upper back. As you perform the stretch, take care not to compromise your spine, leaning back with the weight of your body.

10▶ To make the stretch more active for your partner, he can also entwine his grip around your own. So your partner feels a satisfying stretch, make sure he is relaxed and gives you his full arm weight. As you put your whole body behind your action, this movement will feel equally good for you.

11▶ To lower the arm, keep supporting with your hands and circle it round to the side. Then with his upper arm resting, but still holding the forearm, gently lower the arm to your partner's side.

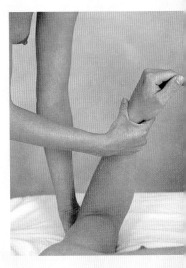

12► Next, holding the wrist, press evenly but firmly with the length of your thumb down the centre of your partner's forearm.

13► As you reach the wrist, use both thumbs to press and make small circles around the bones of the joint.

14◄ Moving outwards from the centre, work your way across the wrist, sliding round to draw down between the tendons of the hand. Pull slowly, drawing tension out between the fingers.

15◄ Turn the hand and circle over the palm with your thumbs. The pressure can be quite firm to feel fully satisfying, while a light stretch between the fingers enhances the sensation.

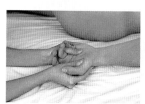

16► Press, twist and squeeze as you pull tantalizingly off each finger. Then repeat the sequence on the other arm.

94

17▲ End gently with soft
caresses with your fingers.

SENSUAL DISCOVERY

As your partner basks in the warmth of the feelings running through his arms, now released, relaxed and sensitized, it is the perfect time for more sensual discovery.

• With your partner's hand turned up towards you, make the gentlest of movements across the palm. Touching and stroking lightly with your fingertips, circle and explore the hand. Trace with your fingers along the lines, closely feeling every fold and crease. Like the face, the hands reflect our world experience, and the way they have been used through a person's life. Close your eyes and let your fingers discover for you. You will feel your partner in a completely different way.

• Using your nails can be an erotically arousing experience. With the tip of your nail, draw across your partner's wrist. The heel of the hand and inner wrist are very sensitive, so there need only be a hint of pressure.

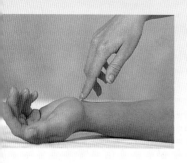

Follow up the inside of your partner's arm, drawing with the nail to the sensitive elbow crease. Keeping the touch intriguingly light and delicate, nails add a dimension to sensation for your partner.

• Explore different ways you can touch each other's arms and hands, using the tips of the nails and fingers, or drawing along the edge. Explore the shape and movement of the forearm, the sensation of the pulse at the wrist. Move up the arm, and feel the contours as the arm rounds into the shoulder. Circle around the uneven and neglected elbow, and return to the familiar roundness of the fingertips. Use your fingers as an extension of your eyes.

• For a change in sensation, blow softly on the palm, altering the shape of your mouth to change the impact. Or circle with your elbow in the centre of the palm, which has a surprising effect of spreading warmth. Caress your partner's arms using your outer forearm, then feel out your partner's body with the backs of your hands.

• As you embrace, be aware of the soft quality in the ways you use your arms. The arms can be used to hold each other close, to encircle and cherish the things we value. If you are still and simply hold your partner's hand, be aware of the feelings that go between you.

THE CHEST

Sit at your partner's head to finish the massage on the upper body. Before starting the massage, look at your partner's body, look at the sensitivity of the breasts, at the openness of the chest, the ribs, the abdomen.

During the massage you will be using both the effleurage technique and stretches to open up the body, pulling up around the ribs and breasts to expand and release the chest.

The main muscles for massage are the pectorals, whose movements are connected to the back. The ribcage, protecting the vital heart and lungs, is also important to massage. The intercostal muscles (between the ribs) work together with the diaphragm, so that the ribcage expands as we breathe in. When breathing is relaxed, the upper chest remains almost still. The breath reaches right to the abdomen when the body breathes naturally.

Feel your partner's vulnerability and sensitivity by placing your hand over the centre of her chest. As the heart pumps blood around the body, massage assists the flow of blood. Keep the strokes sensitive, caressing your partner's body with loving, sensual touches.

CHEST SENSITIVITY
For both men and women, the chest is very erotic, with heightened responses in the nipples and breasts. However, a woman's chest is more sensitive and should be worked around very gently. On a man the pectoral muscles (more accessible on a man than a woman) benefit from releasing massage as they can become quite tight.

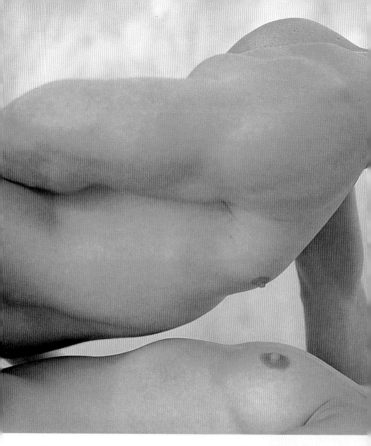

Here, the massage movements can be performed more broadly, the pectoral muscles circled firmly. Then the movements should be brought in closer, the sensitivity of the touch growing greater as the circles decrease.

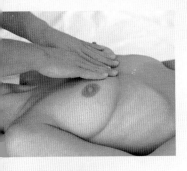

1 ◄ Re-oiling your hands, begin the massage with full effleurage strokes over your partner's chest. Slip down over the breastbone, avoiding pressure to the breasts.

2 ► Without breaking the movement glide your hands over and around the ribs, pulling up just under your partner's body. Give a deep stretch along the ribs, curving your hands softly around the breasts. Return to the top of the chest and complete the movement several times.

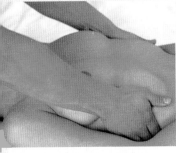

3 ► Then, resting one hand on your partner's shoulder, place the other just under the ribs. Pull up and across towards you, sweeping your hand around the shape of the breast.

4 ► Then push over the pectoral muscles (situated just above the breast), ending the movement at the arm. Repeat on the other side.

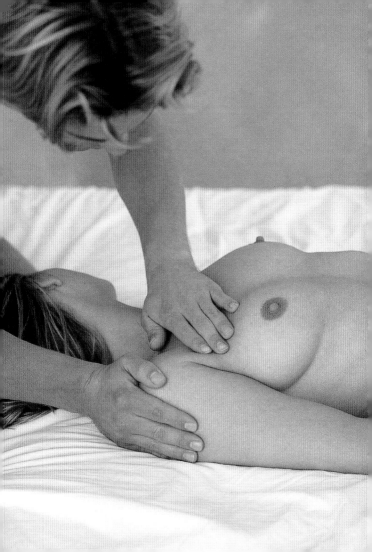

5▲ Place your first two fingers of each hand in the centre of the chest, on either side of the breastbone. With your forefingers under the first rib, and your second fingers in the groove below the next rib, draw firmly outwards, along the curve of the ribs. Ease pressure towards the shoulders.

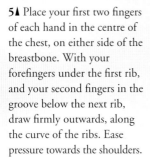
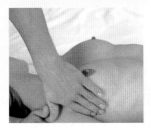

6◀ Supporting with one hand at the shoulder, use your other hand to slide down between your partner's breasts. Carry on with a circle around the breast, gliding your hand underneath.

7◀ Bring your movement round towards the side, and stroking continuously, draw up towards the shoulder. Keep your hands sensitive, light and soft.

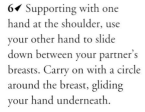

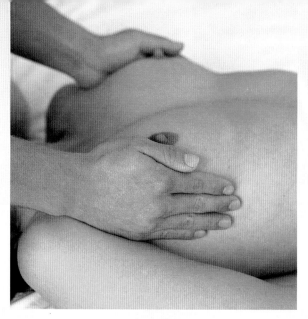

8 ◄ Then bringing your hand back towards the centre, begin to circle around the other breast, to make a figure-of-eight. Change hands if you feel more comfortable and, once more, glide your hand between your partner's breasts.

9 ◄ Follow round and under the curve to pull gently up

the side. Complete the movement several times. Keep your touch close and softly arousing.

10 ▲ Then cup your hands around the breasts. Allow your partner to experience the sensations flowing over her body. These movements are equally as erotic for a man as for a woman.

THE ABDOMEN

Moving naturally down from the chest, the strokes to the abdomen are a completion of the torso massage. Look at your partner's body, notice the curves, the angle of the hips and the unprotected nature of the abdomen. Then from the soft, sensual pelvic area, draw your gaze up along your partner's side. Make your first contact by resting your hands lightly in the centre of his body.

The abdomen is very sensitive and the quality of your first touch will be immediately felt by your partner. Gentle, warming contact with the flat of the hand feels especially good in this area. Always massage in a clockwise direction (following the shape of the large intestine).

The lower abdomen is an important area in terms of inner strength, and being centred here affects our vitality. The abdomen can also be affected by nervous tension and anxiety, which results in feeling weak. For this reason, be even more sensitive than usual when massaging the abdomen, and send positive thoughts through your hands.

FLOWING STROKES
After the initial effleurage you can continue the circling motion of your hands, gradually allowing the pressure to increase. Try and keep the strokes flowing and smooth as your hands cross over each other, expanding the circles slowly to arouse your partner. Knead and pull along your partner's sides, drawing the muscles away from the body. (The large abdominal muscle is the external oblique, under which lie layers of muscles which help in flexing the back.) Be careful not to bring the movement into the

centre. A sideways stretch across the abdomen is good for relieving tension. At the end of the massage softly hold your partner, providing balance, while diffusing the feelings aroused by your strokes. For a man, the abdomen is particularly arousing and sensitive, so keep pressure gentle but firm. For a woman, the area may be quite tender, depending on her menstrual cycle.

As you massage, keep the movements free and sensual, enjoying every bit of your partner's body. The abdomen varies a great deal from person to person. Notice the skin texture, the way the body curves, the hairs covering the skin, the deep relaxing breaths coming down the torso.

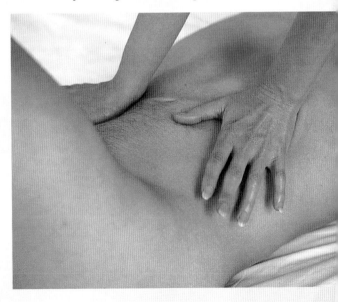

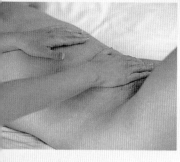

1 ◄ Cover your hands with more oil. Then approaching contact with your partner sensitively, effleurage, moving your hands in a clockwise direction. Let your hands follow the curve of your partner's ribcage.

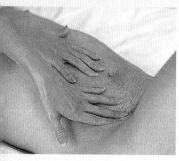

2 ➤ Still circling in the same direction, make your movements a little deeper, pressing with the flats of your hands. As your hands cross over each other, always have one hand continuing to apply the pressure.

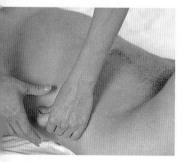

3 ➤ Leaning over your partner, knead the muscles along his side, pulling and rolling the flesh away from the body. Repeat this movement on the other side.

4 ► Then resume the broad circling with your hands. Expand your circles to tantalize him.

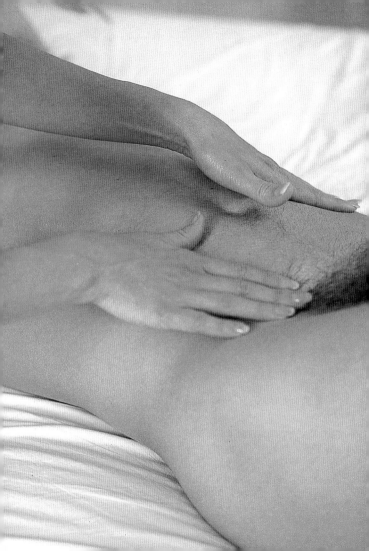

5 After the circling movements, bring your hands softly to the centre of your partner's abdomen and place them together, facing diagonally across the body. Pressing evenly and steadily with the flats of your hands, slowly draw them apart. Bring one hand to the hip and the other to the ribcage, caressing the sides of the body. Then repeat this movement in the other direction. Your strokes should be smooth, gliding and continuous.

6 As you end, place one hand over the abdomen and the other softly underneath the back. This balances your partner and diffuses the surge of feelings, bringing you and your partner very close. Enjoy watching the way your partner's body moves as he breathes.

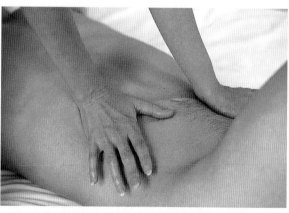

THE FRONTS OF THE LEGS

From the tender work on the abdomen, move on to
the front of your partner's legs, completing the flow of
sensations over the front of the body. Before continuing
your contact, look once more at your partner's legs. From
the delicate shape of the ankle, to the knees and along the
thighs, follow up and over the curve of the hips. Notice
how the legs naturally turn out, coming down to the
softness of the toes. Make your first contact by resting
your hands gently over the top of your partner's feet.

When you begin to effleurage her legs, reach right up
over your partner's thighs, bringing your strokes over and
around the hips. Remember to rock the legs gently on the
downward stroke to loosen the joints and muscles. The
pelvis plays an important part in the movement of the
leg, for if it is contracted, this alters the way the legs are
held. The pelvis can often be thrust back or forwards,
which naturally affects the position of the spine. Very
often sexual feelings become trapped, cutting off
sensations to the legs.

RESTORING ENERGY

The squeezing stroke that you use in this massage
helps to remove waste products from the muscles, and
restores the natural flow of energy. Circling lightly round
the knee cap releases pressure in the joint, sending
pleasurable sensations round the knee. When you come
to massaging the thighs, it is worth realizing that they
contain some of the most powerful muscles in the body
and appreciate firm massage. However, you must ease the

pressure as you approach the knee joint. You will also
need to change your position so that you can reach down
the whole length of the leg. Your partner will absolutely
love this movement.

As you massage, 'listen' to your partner's legs. Try to
ascertain where they need attention. If your partner plays
a lot of sport, for example, the thighs may be particularly
hungry for deep pressure. The feet also enjoy firm
pressure, and the ankles, knees and hips benefit from

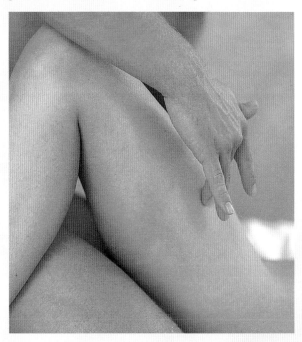

being stretched. Passive movements on the legs feel both liberating and deliciously enjoyable. Giving the entire weight of your body to your partner, let him take responsibility for your limbs. The fronts of your legs adore sensual strokes, especially light touches down the thighs and around the knees. The fronts of the feet and ankles are also extremely sensitive, as are the toes. After the stretching movements, tenderly stroke your partner's legs with long strokes and then softly caress the feet.

When performing the circling and stretches move close in to your partner and you can then move the joints freely. As you rotate the hip, explore the movement of the joint, without exerting pressure on the knee. The hip joint, like the shoulder, a ball and socket joint, is held firmly in place by strong ligaments. As the joint itself is quite deep, these rolls feel particularly rewarding. Be inventive when massaging the fronts of your partner's legs, taking full advantage of their flexibility.

Be very sensitive to your partner, and always check that the pressure feels all right. There is a type of pressure that feels as if it is doing good, and there is another, which is simply pain. The massage movements should never hurt your partner.

RELEASING TENSION

Along the fronts of the thighs run the powerful quadriceps muscles, used in hip and knee movements. Crossing the thigh is the sartorius muscle, the longest muscle of the body. The muscles of the calf affect the movements of the ankle as well as being used to extend the toes. When massaging the calves, work to either side of the shins, as it can be painful pressing directly on the bone. Be sensitive with regard to the knee, which contains thin cartilage between the bones, and while resilient, can sometimes be quite fragile. The knees are also a place where tension is often held. They should remain slightly bent for energy to flow freely.

As well as providing the means for motion, our legs are also our stability. Tension affects the way we stand. When standing, both legs and feet should be relaxed, the feet planted firmly on the ground. You may find that you stand with your toes curled, as if you are gripping on to life. Spend time finding the balance in your stance. Retain an even pressure between the heel and the ball of the foot. Imbalance affects the entire body position.

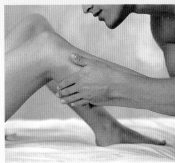

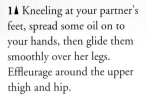

1▲ Kneeling at your partner's feet, spread some oil on to your hands, then glide them smoothly over her legs. Effleurage around the upper thigh and hip.

2◄ Return to press firmly up the calf muscles either side of the bone. Use the heels of your hands for extra pressure.

3◄ Slide the length of your thumbs around your partner's knee, circling and pressing around its shape.

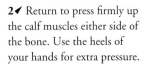

4► Lifting your partner's thigh, squeeze firmly down the muscles, using the heels of

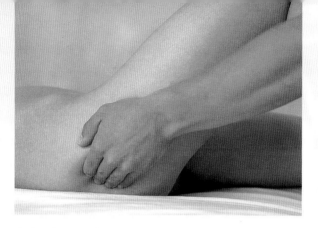

the hands to give firmer pressure. Stroke more gently on the inner thigh.

5▲ With your partner's leg still raised, move your hand towards the hip, and press around the hip joint with

your fingers. Keep the pressure reasonably firm and then press in towards the body, without pressing over the bone. Repeat the movement several times to release tightness around the hips and buttocks.

6◄ Then softly with your fingertips stroke up the back and inner thigh, heightening the arousal for your partner. The delicate strokes over the skin contrast with the movement over the hip, helping to diffuse the strong sensations already aroused.

115

7▶ Rest your partner's thigh over your leg and begin to knead the muscles firmly and deeply. Start the kneading movements at the top of the thigh, gradually working towards the knee. Knead firmly along the front of the leg, rolling the flesh up and away from the bone. In order to penetrate the muscles deeply, use your thumbs to give extra pressure to the rolls. As the muscles can be quite tight here, keep your wrists flexible to allow the maximum movement of your hands. Ease the pressure as the muscles taper towards the knee. Then lower the leg and move to your partner's feet.

8✔ Placing one hand around the heel and the other over the foot, lift your partner's leg and pull slowly back towards you. This stretch reaches along the leg to the hip. Pull back with your arms straight, using the weight of your body, keeping a gradual

pressure until you feel resistance. Then, still holding your partner's foot, lower it gently with your hands. Keep support with one hand under the heel and move the other to your partner's knee.

9▶✔ With one hand beneath the heel and the other at the knee, bend your partner's leg towards her chest.

116

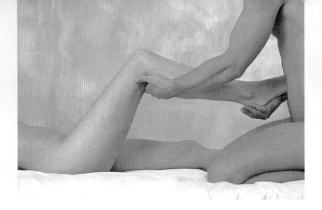

10▲ Supporting her leg, slowly circle it outwards across her body. You will find that the hip opens naturally to the side. The movement affects the hips and lower back.

11▲ Then press your partner's leg towards her chest, giving a stretch along the front of the thigh. Make sure your partner relaxes, surrendering the weight of her leg. Press to the point of resistance, then lower her leg back down slowly.

THE FEET

Now turn your attention wholly to your partner's feet.
Open out the foot by pressing up and pulling across the
bones. This releases the whole foot. (The top of the foot
rarely receives much attention.) Then press the sole of the
foot firmly for deeply relaxing sensations. Hook your
fingers around the toes and give little tugs. Firm pressure
around the toe joints feels instantly satisfying, easing the
pressure around the sensitive instep. As a contrast to the
pressure on your partner's foot, hold the foot softly,
wrapping your fingers around it, and then simply resting
your hands. This focuses awareness down your partner's
body, and provides a feeling of stillness.

REFLEXOLOGY

In a reflexology massage various points on the feet
(which relate to specific areas of the body) can be
massaged to relax and tone its corresponding area of the
body. The theory is that the body is divided into zones,
so the reflex of an organ or structure will be found in the
corresponding zone on the foot. The underside of the
foot follows the shape of the body with the line for the
diaphragm running just below the ball. The waist line
runs across the centre of the foot and the heel line
crosses the heel.

The various parts of the body are then mapped on to
the foot, according to their position. For example, the
toes contain the reflexes for the head, the kidneys are
represented in the centre of the foot, and the spinal
reflexes run along the inside edge. By pressing the foot

you can stimulate a particular part of the body with tender areas designating where tension lies. You may find it valuable to bear these points in mind as you massage your partner's feet. Whatever your movements, be sure your partner will enjoy them.

COMPLETING THE MASSAGE

Spend some time just feeling the sensations between you and your partner, as the feelings flow down your partner's body. All the sensations of the massage are now centred in your partner's feet. Now it is time for soft, gentle caresses and stroking. Your partner will be completely relaxed and at the same time will be experiencing a renewal of her inner vital energy. Spend a little time caressing her feet, pulling and separating the toes. Then draw your hands softly along her feet, perhaps also brushing gently with your lips. Draw the massage to a close, keeping contact with your partner's eyes.

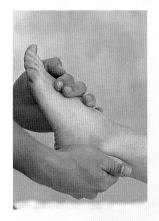

One of the most delightful moments of the experience for you will take place as your partner becomes ready for activity to return the favour. You will soon discover that the pleasure of receiving a massage is highly infectious. Get ready to enjoy this relaxing and sensual time together.

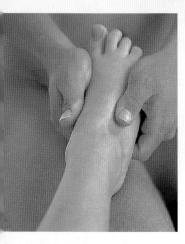

2▼ Supporting the foot, press across the sole with the flat of your thumb, pressing in and then withdrawing pressure evenly. Press firmly round the toes and continue the movement over the heel, but reduce the pressure in the fleshy centre of the foot.

1▲ Rest your partner's leg against your thigh, then place the length of your thumbs together across the foot. Cup your fingers under the sole. Pressing upwards with your fingers, create an arch and draw your thumbs over the top of the foot, moving outwards from the centre. Use the heels of your thumbs to draw the tension out, giving the sense of opening and expansion. Repeat this several times over.

few moments, use gentle brushstrokes down the legs and teasingly bring your hands down over the foot.

4▼ Then softly fold your hands around her foot, keeping your body completely still. This helps to focus sensations, and draws the energy to your partner's feet. When you feel ready, begin the movement sequence on the other foot. This will bring the massage to a close.

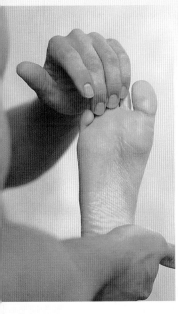

3▲ Still supporting your partner's heel in your hand, curl your fingers underneath her toes. Then, having hooked them around the foot, gently stretch and pull. You may be able to lift the entire foot and shake the toes gently to loosen any tension. Your partner can curl her toes around your hand. After a

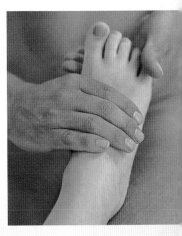

SHARING THE EXPERIENCE

With wonderfully pleasurable sensations flowing all over your partner's body, end the massage with lively, light-hearted strokes.

• Ripple your fingers down the front of your partner's body, tickling and gently teasing her. This will uplift her energy, creating a dynamism between you. Keep the contact constant with your eyes. After lying down for the length of the massage, your partner will probably need a few minutes in order to adjust to movement.

• When ready she should roll over towards her side, then push herself up into a sitting position with her hand. After a massage, whether a relaxing or sensual massage, the whole body feels absolutely sensational, much lighter than before and infused with a profound sense of general wellbeing. Smiles and laughter come naturally. Massage reaches to the very heart of a person, creating special moments for two loving people to share.

123

OILS AND THEIR USES

This is a brief guide to some useful essential oils and their health-giving properties and qualities.

Basil Antiseptic. Nerve tonic. Uplifting. (Avoid during pregnancy.)

Bergamot Antiseptic. Good for skin and respiratory infections. Sedative. Uplifting. (Avoid using neat on skin or in direct sunlight.)

Camomile Soothes inflammation. Relieves aches and pains and dry skin. Sedative. Anti-depressant.

Clary Sage Nerve tonic. Sedative. Good for nervous depression. Helps ease painful periods. Promotes childbirth. Aphrodisiac.

Frankincense Astringent. Relieves catarrh. Soothing. Rejuvenating.

Geranium Skin cleanser and tonic. Mild diuretic. Sedative. Uplifting.

Jasmine Sedative. Anti-depressant. Anti-spasmodic. Relieves period pains. Promotes childbirth. Euphoric. Aphrodisiac.

Juniper Nerve tonic. Astringent and skin tonic. Diuretic. Relieves indigestion. Sedative.

Lavender Antiseptic. Relieves skin inflammation and burns. Relieves stomach complaints. Sedative. Relaxing. The most useful all-round oil.

Marjoram Nerve tonic. Aids digestion. Relieves muscle spasm. Lowers blood pressure. (Avoid using during pregnancy.)

Melissa Tonic. Anti-depressant. Relieves hysteria and palpitations. Regulates menstrual cycle. Uplifting.

Neroli Regenerates the skin. Relieves diarrhoea. Sedative. Anti-depressant. Calming. Aphrodisiac.

Patchouli Stimulant. Astringent. Aids mental clarity. Aphrodisiac.

Rose Antiseptic. Cleansing. Soothing. Promotes circulation. Strengthens digestive system. Relieves stress. Good for mature, dry skin. Aphrodisiac.

Rosemary Antiseptic. Stimulant. Aids mental clarity. Heart tonic. Clears dandruff. Cleansing. Relieves headaches as well as general aches and pains.

Sage Nerve tonic. Diuretic. Relieves general aches and pains.

Sandalwood Relieves dry, inflamed skin, sore throats and coughs. Sedative. Aphrodisiac.

Thyme Antiseptic. Nerve tonic. Relieves headaches and general aches and pains. Stimulates circulation. Invigorating.

Ylang Ylang Lowers blood pressure. Good for oily skin. Aphrodisiac. Sedative. Euphoric. (Use only small quantities.)

MAKING A MASSAGE OIL

Fill a 28ml(1fl oz) bottle three-quarters full with a carrier oil.

Add 5 per cent almond oil. Add a few drops of wheatgerm oil to preserve it (optional). Add 12 drops of an essential oil of your choice. Fill the bottle with grapeseed oil to top up. Use a screw-top bottle and store in a cool place.

Sensual massage oils

Add eight drops of ylang ylang and four drops of neroli or eight drops of sandalwood with four drops of ylang ylang or six drops of jasmine with six drops of rose.

Relaxation after-bathing oil

Add eight drops of lavender and four drops of geranium to a base oil made up of 28ml (1fl oz) of almond oil with 5 per cent avocado oil.

Sensual after-bathing oil

Add seven drops of rose and five drops of neroli.

Stimulating after-bathing oil

Add seven drops of lavender and five drops of rosemary.

MASSAGE CHECK LIST

Oils

Towels

Pillows and cushions

Tissues

Space to move around
your partner

Heating

Soft lighting

Some water

Music (optional)

Answering machine on

An hour when you will not
be disturbed

THE DO'S AND DON'TS OF MASSAGE

As long as you are sensitive and careful, you will not be able to do any harm at all through massage. However, here are a few simple guidelines to help you:

✔ Remember to remove any jewellery before you start a massage and to keep your nails reasonably short.

✘ Do not massage after a heavy meal.

✘ Do not have a hot bath after receiving a massage.

✘ Do not try to cure persistent muscular aches or pains. If your partner experiences any problems or any sharp pains during the massage, consult your doctor or a qualified practitioner.

✘ Do not massage directly on the spine.

✘ Do not massage recent injuries.

Traditionally do not massage:

✘ If your partner has a heart condition.

✘ Over the abdomen in the first four months of pregnancy.

✘ Around or over a tumour.

✘ Over varicose veins.

Always consult your doctor if in doubt.

INDEX

ACKNOWLEDGEMENTS

I would like to thank Dave, Andy, Elizabeth and Neil for their help. And I would also like to thank my teachers and, of course, my massage clients.

Executive Editor **Jane McIntosh**
Editor **Sharon Ashman**
Executive Art Editor **Leigh Jones**
Designer **Louise Griffiths**

Production Manager **Louise Hall**
Index by **Indexing Specialists**
Photographer **Richard Truscott**